WOMAN,
You Are Beautiful

BOYE'S MEMOIR
SERIES 1

BOYE ONALAJA

WESTBOW
PRESS®
A DIVISION OF THOMAS NELSON
& ZONDERVAN

WestBow Press books may be ordered through booksellers or by contacting:

WestBow Press
A Division of Thomas Nelson & Zondervan
1663 Liberty Drive
Bloomington, IN 47403
www.westbowpress.com
844-714-3454

Scripture taken from the King James Version of the Bible.

ISBN: 978-1-6642-5190-8 (sc)
ISBN: 978-1-6642-5189-2 (e)

Print information available on the last page.

WestBow Press rev. date: 12/13/2021

CONTENTS

DEDICATION

This book is dedicated to my dearest mum, Mrs. Juliana Adeyimika Okunsanya in loving memory.

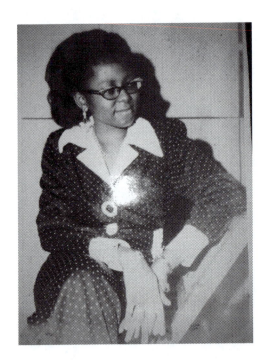

WOMAN, YOU ARE BEAUTIFUL

This is a special message to all women out there and reading this book. A message to let you know that 'You are Beautiful', Woman, you are truly Beautiful'. Regardless of what you have gone through, where you have been, your experiences (good or bad), what has happened to you, or what you have done, you are still beautiful. Your story is your power.... (Michelle Obama). Your true beauty lies within you and can spring forth from the inside out, you just have to try to let it. Your past or situation or mistakes should not define you, they should make you stronger and better, and even more determined to succeed.

You just need to find yourself, and in finding yourself, you discover your worth, your inner core and your inner beauty. Finding yourself can be a very rewarding and fulfilling personal experience, which would help you find that inner peace and joy that lies within you. You can find yourself even through a painful experience. Once found, that beauty will flow from the inside out, and bring out your true beauty. Be willing to share your special gift with others, and spread that beauty to others, making the world a more beautiful place because woman, you are beautiful. Remember 'you are fearfully and wonderfully made' Psalm 139verse14 (King James Version (KJV).

Here is the Legacy Memoir of a beautiful woman who has experienced the ups and downs of life, and has come out stronger, and even more beautiful for it. It is a reflective journey to preserve her most significant memories and life lessons for generations to come. Everybody has a legacy of things they have accomplished or things they have learned just by living life. She shares her journey through life in her memoir, using her life's experiences to leave a legacy for young women, describing how she has been able to navigate through the challenges of life, marriage, motherhood, career, etc.

ONE

My Origin

My full names are Omoboyede Abosede Edoghogho Onalaja (nee Okunsanya). Quite lengthy heh! I have no English names; my father does not believe in giving out English names. I am from the Yoruba tribe in Ogun State, Nigeria, West Africa. The meaning of my names are as follows:

Omoboyede – a child that was born at a time when either of the parents was given a chieftaincy title/religious title. I was born four days after my father was ordained an Archdeacon in the Anglican Communion.

Abosede – a child born on a Sunday. I was born on a Sunday.

Edoghogho – which also means '*ojo ayo*' in Yoruba. The English translation for the name is 'day of joy'. It is a name derived from the Edo tribe in Edo State, Nigeria. The name was given to me by one of my Godmothers, who hails from Owo/Benin in Edo State, Nigeria.

I have a dark birthmark on my back, and as I grow, it grows wider. I am a very simple easy-going person. Though I do not smile too often, but I try as much as possible to be friendly, when I am amid people, but typically I am a very private person.

My mother's pregnancy was pretty much normal and full-term, but I was born at home. I was born at home around 3pm in the afternoon. I was born in Owo, a town in Ondo State, Nigeria, on January 11, 1953. I was like any other baby. I was told I was bubbly, smart and well-behaved as a child. Right from the word-go, I was born into a close-knit family of five, consisting of my mum, dad with three siblings. We were all very close and were practicing Christians. My father was a Reverend of the Anglican Communion, and my mum was a Methodist Lay Preacher before she got married to my Dad. My father's name was Isaac Oyelaja Sonola Okunsanya, and my mother's name was Julianna Adeyimika Okunsanya (nee Akindehinde). My eldest sister was Iyabo Oluwayemisi Okunsanya (she is late now), my older brother is Adegboyega Gordon Okunsanya, and my immediate older sister is Adetokunbo Olubukola Okunsanya. One of my elder brother's godfather was European, and his name was 'Gordon', so he gave my brother the name 'Gordon'. I am the last born of the family. Although I was told my mother lost two children (both girls) in between my eldest sister, Iyabo, and brother, Gordon, and between my brother and my immediate elder sister, Adetokunbo.

As a toddler, I cannot recall ever sleeping in a crib. I slept on a normal bed. At that time, there were no televisions, but we had a gramophone and radio (with only one station). The radio was turned on only in the evenings. We initially lived in a bungalow in Owo, Ondo State, but we later moved to Akure, a neighboring town in Ondo State, because my father was promoted to the post of Archdeacon. We moved into a two-story building in Akure. The house was greyish brown in color, and was built with stones, and it was in a large compound with small single flats at one-end of the compound. The interior of the house was partly light-grey and cream in color. In all the houses we lived in, there was always a small chapel (where we had our prayers daily as a family). In the Akure house, the living room was downstairs, dining room, guestroom and kitchen were also downstairs, while the bedrooms and all the other rooms were upstairs.

I started my Primary Education in Akure at St. Matthias Demonstration School. I attended that school with my immediate older sister, Adetokunbo. My other siblings were already in Secondary/High School at the time, in other states. All this while, my mother was a housewife, but she actively took part in all church programs especially involving women, such as women's guild, and later *'egbe aya bishop'* (meaning bishops' wives' group). She was involved in organizing meetings for them, teaching arts & crafts, cooking, and baking. She taught the women how to cook dishes/meals outside their local dishes. She was a Teacher by Profession, she studied Home Science in school. My mother also used to counsel women who had issues with their husband, children, or husband's family, and being the youngest and last born of the family, in some cases I used to accompany her to such meetings. While at these meetings with my mum, I used to observe and listen intently to everything that was going on or being said.

Being the last born of the family, I used to follow my parents to so many places such as Lagos, Ibadan, etc. I was with my mum most of the time and I learnt a lot from her from the way she related with women, with her husband and how she used to cook and bake. My mother took it upon herself to train all of us (my siblings and I) in the way of the Lord, because my father was always very busy, going about his evangelism mission. But whenever he was around, we had quality time with him, and he also instilled in us the way of the Lord. Every Sunday, when we return from church, my father would ask us what the sermon was about, and what the bible passages read in church were. So, whenever we went to church, we dare not sleep during the service, or let our minds wonder. We would all pray together in the morning and in the evening. Even when he was out of town, my mother, siblings, and I would still pray together. Our parents ensured that we always studied the bible. I was a member of the Choir in our church, St. Davis Anglican church in Akure at the time.

My mother brought up some of her cousin's children, they lived with us growing up. She instilled in us the value and importance of being with family, not just nuclear but also extended if need be. My parents were very nice, kind and welcoming to people, both known and unknown. My parents adopted a son from *Bassa Nkom* (a town in the outskirts of Lokoja, Benue State) and named him Ayodele Okunsanya. So, I have an adopted brother who resides in Nigeria.

Later, my father was ordained a Bishop and we again relocated to Ondo in 1964. At that time, Adetokunbo and myself were in Secondary (High) School; a girls-only school called Fiwasaiye Girls Grammar School, a school founded by my father and the District Education Officers in Ondo Diocese; Late Chief Odukunle and Late Bishop Falope. My siblings and I were very active in church, all through my childhood and adolescence. My parents instilled strong Christian values in us, and this really influenced my lifestyle, my morals, and values.

TWO

Childhood Habits & Lessons

I used to suck my left thumb as a child. I recall that anytime my parents went out, I would cry uncontrollably for hours, because I was very close to my mum. I also loved singing, and making up my own songs or lyrics, and I used to enjoy it which was why I eventually joined the Choir.

I was and I am still left-handed. I remember my first day in school, being left-handed, my teachers noticed this, and asked me not to use my left-hand in class, as it was forbidden in those days in Nigeria. So, when I returned home that day, I told my father, and the following day, my father went with me to school, and told the school authorities not to force me to change. After my father left, they still did not allow me to use my left-hand that much, which is why to this day, I use both left and right-hand to write.

My family and I used to attend church every Sunday, and once or twice during the week for mid-week meetings. When I was about 4 years old, my siblings and I used to visit a stream near the house, it was there I learnt to swim. My parents bought different sizes of bicycles/tricycles (with support at the sides for toddlers) for all of us growing up, my older siblings and some of my relatives who lived with us at the time, taught me how to ride the bicycle.

I love cats and I remember always having lots of cats in the house growing up. After marriage, I had a cat and dog named Bimbo and Shira.

There was a time my mum left something on her dressing table (I cannot really remember what it was), but I remember taking it. Sometime later, she asked for who took it, and initially I did not respond because I was afraid. Later, I confessed that I was the one who took the item, and she beat me and reprimanded me for not telling her immediately. She then said if I take or move any of her things from where it is placed, I should let her know immediately so she will not be looking for it, and to always own up and tell the truth immediately at all times. It hurt me because I loved my mum very much and I never wanted to offend her. That was the first time I did anything to offend her. That experience was my first major lesson in life, and I tried never to offend her again.

Growing up, whenever I attended a funeral with my parents, I would get so scared for days, I would not be able to stay in a dark place alone. Whenever I saw a coffin, I used to be extremely scared, and particularly in dark places. Generally, I used to fear the dark. With age and time, I eventually overcame my fears.

THREE

Adolescence

I attended Fiwasaiye Girls Grammar School in Akure, for my secondary education. It is a single-sex (girls-only) school. Most of my teachers were European Missionaries except one who was a Peace Corp member from America, Ms. Anderson. I was made a prefect in high school. I got confirmed to become a full-fledged member of the Anglican Church, in the school chapel at the age of fifteen. My father, being a Bishop at the time, came to conduct the Confirmation ceremony (as it was called). When you are confirmed in the Anglican Church, that is when you can receive holy communion in church. The students that were being confirmed were allowed to wear special 'white' dresses for that day, and I wore a lacey white flowery dress, made by my mum, with a matching hat. My mother used to sew. My mother brought some snacks and drinks for my friends. After the Confirmation ceremony, we entertained my friends with the refreshments, and at the end of the day, my parents returned home.

Back in those days, full dresses were in vogue for children, short-skirts and bell-earrings for women, and baggy trousers for men. This was in the late sixties. From childhood to my teenage years, I used to plait my hair with black thread, and sometimes weave/cornrow it. I had very long black hair. I did not retouch my hair until after I had finished high school. Back then, highlife music was in vogue, and I used to enjoy listening to it.

In high school, the school food was quite good, but it was served in small portions. They used to serve us 'eko' (pap pudding) on Tuesdays and Thursdays, the 'eko' they used to serve on Tuesdays was not so good, but the one served on Thursdays was a lot better. It was usually served with vegetables (spinach) – 'efo'. Sometimes I used to swap food with my friends, particularly when I did not like the food being served very much. I was a member of the Literary and Debating society. I used to participate in an activity in school called 'catching the train'. It is an activity where different apparels; be it blouses, trousers, or shoes) are placed in the field 50 yards apart. You wear the first apparel, then you run to the next part of the field, until you are fully dressed. At the start of the game, you are expected to be in your underwear (or sports dress), but by the time you finish the race, you are expected to be fully dressed. Once you put on your last apparel, you run to the finish line. The first person to get to the finish line comes first, and the 2nd person to get to the finish line, comes 2nd, and on and on like that.

My school (Fiwasaiye Girls Grammar School) is situated on the outskirts of town, more or less in a forest. There were no residential houses around the school apart from our classrooms and dormitories then. We had something like a well or spring water source where clean water comes out and where we get water to drink, bathe or wash our clothes. We basically used the water for everything. The water was so nice, clean, and safe to drink. The school built a small shelter on top of the well. There was no way we could have pipe-borne water because the school was located in a forest.

I came first twice in English Language in high school. I remember receiving two prizes (books) for coming first in English Language. English was my best subject, followed by Music. Chemistry however was my worst subject because I found it difficult to understand and I also found it quite confusing. I was a member of the School Choir, I recall a time when we travelled to Ibadan, Oyo State, to sing for another school; I used to sing 'soprano'. We also had a choir festival whereby a choir from another school came to join us for a choir recital, bringing guitars, cello, trumpets, flutes, and all sorts of musical instruments. We had a great time, and the other students from other schools came to watch us perform.

Around that time, Ms. Davies, my Music teacher, noticed my interest in Music, and enrolled me for a Certificate Music program at the Royal School of Music England. She also taught me how to play the piano. I took the exams (parts 1, 2 and 3) and passed all the stages. I was awarded three certificates for the different parts, so I know how to play the piano very well, how to read the keys and play accordingly. That was what encouraged me to join the choir in my church much later. Ms. Davies was my favorite teacher; she was very caring and inspiring. She also taught us Religious Knowledge.

I used to hang out with Folake, Chika and Jumoke in high school. Jumoke was very brilliant and athletic; though she was chubby, she still used to come first in the 100m and 200m relay races, and she used to represent the school in the Inter-house sports.

Chika was also brilliant, and somewhat athletic, she used to play basketball. She was also very beautiful and friendly. She was from the Eastern part of Nigeria. She stayed with my family during the school holidays. During the Civil War, the Ibos were returning to their states because they wanted to return to their homes to be with their families. While they were running away, Chika stayed with my family for a while, but when the war was getting more serious, her father sent for her to return to the village as soon as possible, so my father arranged for someone to take her to Ore, a neighboring village, and from there, someone was asked to take her to Umuahia, Anambra State, where her family was. Since that time, I have not seen Chika, and I really miss her. We lost contact thereafter.

Folake is a light-skinned beautiful girl; very friendly and intelligent. She also used to come first in English Language, both of us actually used to compete for '1st' position in English Language. At a point, my cousin wanted to marry her, but things did not work out between them. Folake later moved on to Ilorin, where she worked at the University of Ilorin as a Registrar for so many years. We are still in touch till this day. I am also very much in touch with Jumoke. She is actually my best friend. She is like a sister to me. I was her maid-of-honor at her wedding.

My first date was with my cousin's friend, Bosun (I cannot remember his last name). I had just finished high school at the time. Bosun toasted (wooed) me and approached me for a relationship, we dated each other for a short-while. Bosun had a chocolate-colored complexion, he was of medium height, and was handsome, funny, and witty. He was quite the charmer. He was slightly taller than me. The relationship was however short-lived because I felt I wanted someone more mature, and Bosun was not really mature, so I called off the relationship.

Later, I met Segun, who was dark in complexion and of medium height, and was nice and caring. He was studying at the University of Ibadan, Oyo State, Nigeria at the time. At that time, my parents had moved away from Akure, to Ondo because my father had become a Bishop so during our mid-term breaks, instead of going to Ondo, my parents used to ask me to spend the long weekend with their family friends, Segun's family. Segun and his parents were our family friends. His parents lived in Akure, and his father came to replace my father in Akure as the Archdeacon of Akure Diocese. During one of those mid-term breaks, he approached me for a relationship and told me he liked me. I told him 'I will think about it'.

In my interactions with Segun, it seemed like he wasn't really straightforward, but he kept convincing me that he really cared for me. Then, we started dating each other.

A few months later, after Segun had completed his first Degree at the University of Ibadan, he travelled to the United Kingdom, while I moved on to Christ's School, Ado-Ekiti to do my A 'Levels. I was there for only two terms, and then I returned home to take my NCE (National Certificate of Education) exams. All this time, we were still going steady in the relationship, and keeping in touch. During the Summer holidays, my immediate older sister, Adetokunbo travelled to London on vacation. She intimated me of a few things she found out about Segun, that I wasn't too pleased about, so I ended the relationship immediately. It was very painful for me because he was the first man I fell in love with, so I thought to myself…'can I trust again?'. My heart was broken, and it took me quite a while to get over him.

The experience sort of made me wary of men and affected my trust in men generally. I rebuffed all my subsequent suitors, and lost interest in men and dating in general. Luckily for me, our relationship was not consummated. Though he had tried to have sex with me, and hinted it on many occasions, but I told him I wanted to save my body for my wedding night.

Growing up, I always wanted to become a nurse because I like caring for people, taking care of them, making them happy and comfortable. But the issue was that I could take care of people, but as soon as they die, I run away. Since I discovered that I had this fear, I changed my mind and decided to become a teacher instead.

One of my dad's drivers taught me how to drive. We had then moved to Ibadan and my father had retired and I was taking my NCE exams at this time, I was in my late teens. He encouraged me to learn with a stick-shift (manual) car as opposed to an automatic geared car, because at that time, the stick-shift was common. After I had learnt how to drive a manual geared (or stick-shift) car, then I started to drive automatic-geared cars. I used a Peugeot 504 car (my dad's car at the time) to learn driving.

Life lessons I learnt as a teenager:

➢ You do not need to mingle with the crowd, be watchful of the people you hang around with
➢ Do not stay out too late into the night, because my father did not tolerate this at all while my siblings and I were growing up
➢ When you attend a party and you have a drink (or are taking a drink) and you must leave your seat and drink to go to the restroom or dance floor to dance, do not take that drink again when you return to your seat. It is not wise to take the same drink again.
➢ Do not be too close to strangers.
➢ Pay attention to your dressing and be well-groomed. Your clothes should always be clean.

FOUR

My Youthful Years /
My Young Adult Years

After I finished high school, I went to Christ's School to do my HSC (Higher School Certificate) exam, for two terms. During my Secondary School Certificate Exam (SSCE), I did not pass Chemistry and Geography, so I could not continue with the HSC. My father encouraged me to go for the NCE (National Certificate in Education) program which was very much in line with my dream job – being a teacher. So, my parents and I decided that I should enroll for the NCE program at University of Lagos.

Meanwhile between Christ's School and University of Lagos, I worked briefly at Oyo State Secretariat, Ministry of Establishment as a Clerical Assistant staff. I worked there for about six months prior to gaining admission at University of Lagos. At the time, my father had retired, and we had relocated to Ibadan, Oyo State, Nigeria. I had a colleague then, who had just completed her High School Certificate exam, her name is Ms. Tokunbo Shomolu. Tokunbo is a nice, gently lady, easy going and quiet, not very outspoken. We were assigned the same duties, and we worked in the same department at the Secretariat. I later left the Secretariat for the University of Lagos, and she left for University of Ibadan, and we lost contact after that.

My first real job was my job at the Oyo State Secretariat. I was responsible for ensuring that Pensioners were paid as and when due, and for managing their respective accounts. I was a punctual employee, never late and was very thorough in executing my duties. I learnt a lot from my dad, he was a strict disciplinarian who never gave room for laziness or idleness in the office for his staff. I observed this anytime I visited him at his office. Even at home, he never condoned laziness, whenever it was time for homework, we had to do it. He strongly believed that there was a time for everything, and everything had to be done at the right time. This discipline was instilled in us and remains with me and all his children till this day.

This is not to say that I am completely perfect, I had my own shortcomings. Whenever anyone passed a negative comment or remark about my job at work, it hurt me a lot and I would withdraw and go quiet for a while, and then try to avoid the person. I guess that was my weakness. Sometimes I would confide in my colleague and friend, Ms. Tokunbo Shomolu about it.

After a few months of working at the Ministry, I went back to school (University of Lagos) to do my NCE (National Certificate of Education) Program. Prior to my admission to the University of Lagos, my ex-high school boyfriend, Segun tried to stage a come-back, but I refused him. Once bitten...twice shy. While I was studying at University of Lagos (Unilag for short as we used to call it), I met a young man called Bayo, and he used to take my roommate and I to the movies. He approached me for a love relationship, and I told him that I did not want us to ruin the friendship we shared. I remember he was in Hostel Hall 3, while I was in Hall 5 at the time. He was short, dark-skinned, and rather handsome, but not as handsome as Segun. He was quite lively and jovial, but he was not really my type, plus I was not ready to get into any relationship at that time.

About a year later, while I was still in Unilag, my cousin, Titi and I went to Lagos Island to do some shopping. On our way there, she asked that we make a quick stop at Shomolu to see her Mathematics lesson teacher (someone who coaches her Mathematics at the time). It turned out to be the Onalaja's family house. It was a three-story building in Shomolu, cream and dark brown in color, and the person we went to see was on the 3rd floor. On reaching there, we were directed to the living room in the apartment. It was a small sitting-room, with a recliner, a settee and 2 dining chairs and a small dining table. There were also one or two stools, and there was another door at the back close to where we sat, which led to the balcony. It seemed quite cozy. About three minutes after we sat down, a young man came out of the door opposite where we sat. Titi and the man greeted each other, and they spoke briefly. He then went back to the bedroom, and brought out an exercise book, and gave it to Titi and bade her goodbye. I noticed that he did not even greet or acknowledge my presence.

When we got outside, I told my cousin that I noticed that the guy we went to meet did not even greet me or say hi or hello to a lady, he only greeted one and completely ignored the other. Then I said to my cousin, "He must be an arrogant man", little did I know that he would later become my husband. We then proceeded to Lagos Island to do our shopping and returned home afterwards.

I did not hear anything about him for a while after that, except his name because my cousin told me. When my cousin told me his first and last name – Adekunle Onalaja, and that his parents had been in Ondo State a few years before (in the late sixties), I then put two and two together and recalled that my mother used to discuss cake-making with his mum because his mum was in St Helen's Teacher Training College at the time. I remember his mum used to ask my mum if I was dating anyone and my mum responded saying, "You know these children of nowadays, you can never tell with them". Then she further explained to her that I recently broke up with the person I was dating before, and she was not sure if I was currently dating anyone.

A few years later, both families relocated to Ibadan and both our parents used to visit one another occasionally. Then one day, Adekunle and his bosom friend, Gbenga came visiting and asked to see me. I entertained them, and he expressed his undying love for me, and interest in marrying me. By this time, he was studying abroad in America, and had only come home on holiday. His friend also put in a good word for him, asking me to please consider his friend. But I said to Adekunle, "I think we are related, let me ask my mum first". After they had left, I asked my mum whether we were related, and my mum said, "we are not related, but both families are very close". But I was trying to be very careful because of my past experience, so I did not give Adekunle a direct response then.

Before Adekunle returned to the United States, he informed me that he would be returning to the United States, but he will stay in touch with me. About a month later, his sister, Mojisola and his mum came visiting me and my mum. There was a time they came to our house and explained at length that we were not related at all. They were very nice to me because they really wanted me to date their brother and son. They later invited me for Dinner at their house. I was impressed by their actions, and whenever I visited them, they were warm and kind to me, including their dad who does not really talk much, but he was still very pleasant. Then Adekunle and I started dating each other across the ocean, we communicated through letters and telephone. What really attracted me to my husband was his jovial nature, and his character. Whenever you take something so seriously or are worried about something, he has a way of making light of the situation, and making you feel better about it. He was slim, not too tall with an afro haircut, and was very amiable. I later discovered that he is also a very nice person.

Life lessons I learnt as a young Adult

> You should endeavor to be disciplined and focused in life, know what you want out of life and try as much as possible to achieve it.

Initially I wanted to become a nurse, but when I discussed my fear of dead bodies with my dad, he said, "Well, then you might not be a good nurse, because a nurse must be able to look after someone even after death, you will need to prepare the body for the mortuary". He then suggested I become a teacher instead, since I will still be caring for people – both children and adults, and I agreed with him. So, I refocused my career plan to 'Teaching', stuck with it and never looked back. I later became a successful teacher.

> ➤ In life, you should also endeavor to be resourceful, not limiting your skills to book knowledge alone.

Growing up, I used to watch my mum do a lot of things around the house such as changing the light bulb, screwing loose knots, and other handyman stuff, and I learnt all these by observing and watching her. It made me quite independent. Being the last born, my dad was quite old as I was growing up, and so there was a limit to what he could do, so my mum had to do a lot of the technical stuff in the house.

> ➤ You need to think less of yourself and think more of others. Again, this is one of the lessons my mum taught me.
> ➤ You should endeavor be respectful and mindful of how you talk to others.

FIVE

Family Pedigree

My father's full names are Isaac Oyelaja Sonola Okunsanya. He was born in Lagos on December 13, 1900. He was an Educationist and a Clergyman. My father was the first Anglican Bishop in the whole of Iperu-Remo, Ogun State, Nigeria. He used to play Lawn Tennis, particularly when we were living in Owo, Ondo State, Nigeria. He loved music and helping people. He was a philanthropist. He was firm and a strict disciplinarian and he was godly. I think I took that from him. He was very tall, lanky, well-built, dark-skinned, and handsome. He detested lies; people telling lies. One thing I inherited from him was his height, his generosity, and his complexion.

Lessons I learnt from my father are as follows:

> ➢ You should be firm and always stand for what is right.
> ➢ You should always be able to stand by your word.
> ➢ You should always be genuine.

I admired the fact that he was very gentle and committed to all his children, though firm. And I liked the way he interacted and related with his sub-ordinates, and how he related with my mum. I never saw my parents fight; they never had any noticeable arguments. He was a very loving and caring husband, from my observation. Sadly, he is late now. I was born when my father was in his fifties, and being the last born, I was treated like a pet – 'daddy's pet'. My immediate older sister and I were very free with him, unlike my much older siblings who were a bit scared of him because of his stern nature.

My mother's name is Juliana Adeyimika Okunsanya. (nee Somoye - Akindehinde). She was born on June 1, 1910 in Ago-Iwoye in Ogun State, Nigeria. She was a Teacher by profession before she got married. She was also an accredited Lay Preacher in the Methodist Church Nigeria. She used to sell fashion hats and fabric materials imported from England, and handwoven materials for ladies. She was a fantastic cook, and she was very good with tutoring. She used to tutor her younger relatives (nieces, nephews) and children. She also loved baking. That was how I learnt how to bake and cook.

I resemble my mother very much; my stature and facial appearance, except for my height and complexion which I inherited from my father. One important thing I learnt from her is always to be tolerant and patient. I appreciated her gentleness and tolerance, because her sister-in-law were quite difficult to get along with, but my mother tolerated them and somehow managed to get along with them. Unfortunately, she is late now.

My father went to visit his cousin at United Methodist College for women in Ibadan, and he met his cousin's friend, who attended the same college, in the room. She (being my mum) greeted them, and she left the room. Then, my father told his cousin that he liked her friend. That was how my parents met.

We were a warm closely-knit family, everyone looked out for one another. I had a very good life growing up. Growing up, my two much older siblings (the first two) were always away in school, so I did not really live with them. One was in high school, while the other was abroad (in the United Kingdom). Later, the one in high school went abroad to join my sister who was already abroad. So, I grew up mainly with my immediate older sister, Adetokunbo. Though, the first two used to visit home during the holidays.

The oldest person in my family just died this year – 2020, she was the oldest in my mother's family. She was my mother's younger sister. Her name was Rachael Oladunke Odunlami (nee Somoye-Akindehinde) alias 'Mama Oluyoro'. She died at the age of 103 years. She was strong and active till she died, except for her failing sight. I visited her during my trip to Nigeria in 2018 with my immediate older sister, Adetokunbo at her home in Ijebu-Ode, Ogun State, Nigeria.

I have another aunt (on my father's side); my father's younger sister who had a nursery, primary and secondary school. Her name was Mrs. Tanimowo Ogunlesi (nee Okunsanya). The nursery and primary school were called 'Children Home School'. It was the first boarding nursery and primary school in West Africa. She went on to add a Secondary School, named Christ High School, which was also a boarding school. They are all located in Molete, Ibadan, Oyo State, Nigeria.

My mother's sister, Mrs. Esther Arinola Adenuga-Taiwo was my guardian in Lagos, while I was studying at the University of Lagos. I used to stay in her house during the holidays. She treated me as my own mum would treat me. She was a very soft person, but firm in some ways. But all in all, she was kind and caring. She is late now. The other person that influenced my life was Mrs. Dorcas Osisami (nee Somoye-Akindehinde). After my mother passed, she would visit me and advise me, using her life's experiences as an example. She would tell me everything going on in her life, and even solicit my own advice. We grew to be very close to each other, particularly after my mother died.

My two aunties (mentioned above) and one of my uncles (my mother's youngest brother) were my favorite relatives. My uncle's name was Mr. Olayiwola Akindehinde. He was a Psychiatric Nurse, who was trained in London, and later retired. Upon his retirement, he built a motel, his wife was a caterer. The hotel is called 'Crimson Arcade' and it is situated at Gbagada, Lagos State, Nigeria. He took myself and my husband like his younger sister and brother. His home was always open to us. We were very close. He had our interest in mind.

I have also had the opportunity to mentor some of my younger relatives, and my husband's relatives. I taught them what to expect in life as a woman, before and after marriage. I counselled them on the ups and downs of marriage, and how to overcome them. I also taught them the value of good morals.

SIX

Marriage and Parenting

I got married on August 8th, 1975. It was a bright sunny Saturday morning in August, everything was bright, I had a lovely bouquet of fresh flowers made by a Jamaican florist who had a garden in her compound. She used to sell the flowers to brides getting married or for special occasions. The bouquet was very beautiful, it was a mixture of lilac and cream. All my bridesmaid had one rose that matched the color of their dresses. I wore a nice flowing white lacey gown (with a very long veil) which my sister-in-law, Jean Okunsanya, had bought from London, United Kingdom. She also styled my hair and did my make-up. My husband and his bestman wore a light blue tuxedo with a bow tie and matching shoes. He had an afro haircut and he looked handsome. My cousin, Titilayo was my maid-of-honor, and one of my husband's friends, Seth Runsewe was our best man.

My husband is a medium-built handsome man, and he is a nice man, caring, loving and devoted. He is outgoing, laughs and chats a lot, and makes friends very easily. He is also Godfearing. Whenever I am worried about something, he has a way of making light of the situation. He has a way of solving problems easily. He is also exceptionally brilliant. He is a successful pharmacist, and he runs his own pharmacy. He is also a philanthropist, who loves to give and help people. He is generous to a fault, he does not know how to say no.

We had the traditional wedding ceremony (the engagement) at my parent's house in Felele, Ibadan, Oyo State on a Friday. Then, the following day, we had the Church Wedding service at St. James Cathedral in Oke-Ado, Ibadan, Oyo State, followed by the wedding reception ceremony at Obisesan Hall at Okebola, Ibadan, Oyo State, Nigeria. About a week later, we travelled to Europe, and from Europe, we travelled to Miami for our honeymoon. It was a very lovely and blissful time for us, we really enjoyed ourselves. Our honeymoon was just a few days, but it was nice.

After the honeymoon, we went to Houston, Texas where my husband was studying at the Texas Southern University and began a new life. We had wanted to wait for some time before having children, because my husband was still studying at the time, but there was pressure from my husband's family members who wondered why I had not gotten pregnant yet. So, months after we got married, we decided to have children. I have five children in all, namely: Oluwafemi Onalaja who was born in 1976, Olaide Akinribido (nee Onalaja) born in 1979, Oluwabusola Ajibola (nee Onalaja) born in 1983, Taiwo and Kehinde Onalaja (twins) both born in 1987.

When Oluwabusola (my third born) was born, she was very small at birth, but she was the first one (of all my children to talk). She spoke first at the age of seven months, and she started walking a few weeks after. Olaide used to cry a lot, she never wanted me to put her down (not even for a minute). She wanted to be carried all the time. She never allowed anyone else to hold or carry her except her mum. She walked first at the age of one year and a few weeks. The twins are very identical, and they came into the world fifteen minutes apart; one came at a quarter to 12:00midnight, and the other came at exactly midnight (at the next contraction). They had only one placenta, that was divided only by a thin line. They were very cute and adorable; they used to sleep at the same time, eat and wake up at the same time. They always wanted to do everything together. As they grew older, we noticed that one of them (Kehinde) is left-handed, while the other (Taiwo) is right-handed. Oluwafemi was born naturally, and he was a gently baby. His birth weight was 3.7kg.

I ensured that I knew all my children's friends, at least almost all, because I did not want them to join any bad gang. When Femi went to Secondary School in Jos – Federal Government College, Jos, there was no law and order in the school, seniors maltreated juniors and used to snatch their provisions from them. The stole everything Femi took to school, including his mattress, so he was made to sleep on the bare bed spring. And Jos is a very cold place, so you can imagine how cold and uncomfortable he must have been. So, he returned home with two different slippers, and he only had his school uniform (which he was wearing). Right there and then, I decided that my son would not return to that school, so myself and my husband started looking for a good school. We ended up finding International School Ibadan in Oyo State, Nigeria. Since my mum was living in Ibadan, Oyo State, she said she will be monitoring and visiting him from time to time. He then took the test for entry into Form 2 (2nd year in Secondary/High School) and he passed so he enrolled and started in Year 2 at International School Ibadan, and that was where he completed his Secondary school education.

Since he was there, we encouraged his sister, Olaide to take the entrance exam to the same school, after she completed her elementary education. Olaide also enrolled and was admitted into International School Ibadan, where she also completed her Secondary school education.

Oluwafemi, my first born is a born leader because he is calm (even when under pressure), loving and amiable. Even though he has gone through some challenges in life, he is still a calm person and good leader. He is a good father to his son, Olaoluwaseeni, and a loving and caring husband to his wife, Damilola. He talks to and advises his siblings in a very nice way.

Olaide is a reserved person, anyone who sees her would think she is very reserved and quiet, but when you get closer to her, you will know that she is not that reserved. She is someone you can really relate with, she is very warm, nice, friendly, and cheerful. Olaide is very emotional, she gets hurt easily. But one thing I admire about her is that when someone is hurting, she tries to soothe your feelings, and she tries to make everyone happy. She is very caring. She does not want to see you sad or worried, and I love her for that.

Oluwabusola is a good listener, she will listen to you, she will feel your pain and she will offer her kind words of advice in her own way. She will try as much as possible to lighten your mood, that is Busola. Everyone needs a listening ear from time to time, when you have something bothering you, and you have someone to listen to you, it takes away half of the burden. Oluwabusola is a very nice lady, she is also very diplomatic, she knows how to play around myself and her dad, so that neither of us feel offended whenever we do not agree on a matter.

Taiwo and Kehinde though they are twins, have different attributes. Kehinde generally takes things lightly, he does not take things too deeply (despite the seriousness of the situation), just like his dad. Meanwhile, Taiwo does not talk too much, so you never know what is on his mind. You must more or less force it out of him, he is very deep but also warm and loving. But you may not know this, until you get close to him. Kehinde on the other hand is very outspoken and speaks his mind. He is also caring, open and friendly. He like to claim he is the last born of the family, so any time his brother tries to prevent him from taking something, he would say, "I am the last born, so I can take anything I want in this house".

I try to shower all my five children with the same affection. I have no favorites; I love them all equally. While I was growing up, family togetherness was more pronounced and practiced back then; we used to pray together in the mornings, and evenings (devotion). But when I was raising my children, we did not have time to get together in the morning or even in the evening because it was either their dad does not return home on time, so we could not always all be together to pray together. I was always around but when the head of the family is not back, we could not go ahead to pray and leave him out. But on Sundays, we used to pray and eat together, and most evenings.

Here are some of my parenting tips for the next generation. Please note that I give these tips not because I consider myself an expert in parenting matters, but only by virtue of my experiences as a parent:

➤ Ensure you know what your children are up to as much as possible, particularly nowadays with the advent of Social Media; Facebook, Instagram, snapchat, etc. Ensure you know what is on their social media platforms.

➤ Encourage your children to bring home their friends so that you will know the kind of people they are moving or hanging out with.

➤ Teaching your children, the importance of Etiquette is key;

➤ For girls, their dressing must not expose their bodies much, they must not wear clothes that are too revealing. There is a saying which goes, "How you dress is how you will be addressed".

➤ For boys, no sagging pants.

➤ Personal Hygiene is very key. It is important to teach them:

➤ To use deodorant or anti-perspirant spray daily.

➤ To bathe once or twice daily.

➤ To brush twice daily.

➤ Cleaning and washing their bathing sponge and tooth brush is also vital. For the toothbrush, this can be cleaned weekly or every two (2) weeks. The cleansing can be done by soaking the toothbrush in hot water and mouthwash or listerine, cleaning and rinsing it afterwards. Also, tooth brushes must be changed every three (3) months.

➤ For the bathing sponge, this can also be cleaned every one(1) or two(2) weeks, by soaking in hot water and antibacterial soap or Dettol, cleansing and rinsing afterwards. Typically, bathing sponges must be changed every 3-6 months.

➤ Table manners – teach them how to eat decently, and how to comport oneself when dining with others (at the table). Examples of table manners are "Don't talk with food in your mouth", and using the words "excuse me, could you please pass me the …" whenever you would like someone to pass something to you at the table, amongst others

➤ Endeavor to educate your children on what is right and wrong. They must know what not to indulge in, for instance, not taking other people's things without their permission, young female children or young teenagers hanging out with boys or men. Parents should be weary of that, especially nowadays. There must be rules.

➤ When dealing with a difficult child, tell God your concerns about the child, and God will show you the way to go about it.

➤ Have a nice chat with the child, tell him or her where she went wrong, and the consequences of his/her actions. Try to avoid always scolding the child. Instead try withholding certain privileges from the child as a way of punishment when the child does something wrong.

➤ It is also important to teach your children to be always well-behaved, particularly when they go out with friends, either to a party or anywhere, meaning no foul language, no smoking or hard drugs. I used to educate my kids on the dangers of taking hard drugs.

➤ Try to ensure that your children are free enough with you to discuss anything or any issues they might have bothering them.

➤ When it comes to choosing a life-partner, always guide them on the attributes they should look for in a life-partner.

It is not about how rich or handsome/beautiful the person is, what is more important is that the person is well-behaved. They should look out for the person's personality. Is the person the 'grab-grab' kind, the demanding type, or the possessive type? They should be weary of these things. They should not be carried away by looks alone, they should look more for the person's inner beauty.

Most importantly, ensure that you instill the fear of God into your children, by teaching them biblical principles and morals. Teach them in the way of the Lord.

SEVEN

Places I Have Been To

The places that I have visited are Hong Kong, Taiwan, Luton (in England), Switzerland, Spain, Italy, Dubai, Germany, Canada, London, France, Chicago, and Colombia (in South America). Hong Kong is a metropolitan area located in Asia, with lots of sky-rise buildings, most of which are from ten floors and above. There was a time I visited Hong Kong, and they had the 'typhoon' – a very strong wind that could blow away cars and trucks, lorries, and buses except structures like houses. I recall during one of my visits to Hong Kong, that on this particular day, there was a Television and Radio announcement that a typhoon would occur for the whole day, the next day, and that everyone should be prepared because there will be absolutely no movement at all. Vehicles were caged in very strong iron poles because of the oncoming typhoon. The vehicles were caged inside the welded strong iron rod/poles, so that they would not be blown away by the typhoon. On the day before the typhoon, I wanted to go to a nearby restaurant close to my hotel, and as I walked to the restaurant, the strong typhoon wind started blowing, I had to stay close, cling to the walls, and hold on to the walls tightly until I got to the restaurant to avoid being blown away by the typhoon. I had to buy all the foods and drinks I would need for the whole day, then I returned to my hotel room.

Hong Kong is an interesting place; they can manufacture almost anything within 24 hours. For instance, if you want shoes or clothing made for you within 24 hours, they will make it for you. Most things are very cheap in Hong Kong; clothes, shoes, umbrella, anything you can think of. They have downtown Hong Kong, which is called 'Kowloon', where you can get things wholesale.

Italy is a very lovely place, but you have to be careful because there are so many thieves there. Italy is one place where they sell good Gold; 18-carat, 24-carat, and they also sell good quality leather bags, shoes, belts, and nice skirts. Italy has small towns and villages, but they have a rich culture and nice hotels. They hardly speak English, most of the time they speak their own language, 'Italo'. Their main food is Pasta and cheese, hard bread and pizza.

Switzerland is a beautiful country with lots of landscapes everywhere. The landscaping there is superb, making the country very beautiful. The country is well planned, and the roads are clean, nice and tarred, with lots of beautiful houses. It is a very rich country.

Luton is a small modern town in England, where most of the indigenes are entrepreneurs and are very enterprising. My mum used to buy hats from there (ladies' and men's hats) because they make the hats from scratch. They have a deeper dialect from the usual 'English' Language. They are mostly private people, and their main occupation is manufacturing.

Dubai is an extra-ordinarily nice place, once you arrive in Dubai, you would know instantly that it is a very rich country. Because of the wealth they derive from their Oil, they have been able to develop the whole country. They have sky-scraper buildings and hotels, they have a spectacular hotel built right in the middle of the sea, it is on an island. They are also presently constructing a hotel with rotating floors; in such a way that each floor can rotate on its own, it is due to be completed this year – 2020. Dubai is a very beautiful place, which is constantly developing. They have boat cruises on artificial water, and they have large, lovely malls. They also have a lot of good Gold, particularly in a place called 'Gold Souk', a popular gold market in Dubai with lots of merchants who sell Gold. There are also lots of tourist attractions such as Dubai Fountain, Jumeirah (a newly developed area in Dubai where they have a lot of big hotels, apartment buildings, and other tall buildings). Their main language is the 'Arabic' language.

In Colombia, they speak mostly Spanish, and hardly any English. Colombia was founded by a combination of Blacks, Spanish, and British people. They are very friendly people, and their culture is like the culture in Africa. One of their traditional attires is like a multi-colored gown – white, yellow, red, and grey which is big and flowing with a head -tie (from the same material). They have a market where they sell cooked food, and they also sell yams and roasted corn, where buyers would come and haggle over price, just like in Nigeria. Their roads are very narrow, there is no way two cars can drive side by side on the road. The town is an ancient old-fashioned town. I went there in 2019 for my nephew's 50th birthday.

I remember travelling with my three kids (Oluwafemi, Olaide and Oluwabusola) to Europe and the United States of America a few decades ago. We travelled to London, New York and Chicago. The twins were not yet born at the time. London is the largest city in England and the United Kingdom. There are lots of tourist attractions in London. My children and I visited Madam Tussauds, shopping malls, Selfridges, London West-End – Oxford Circus, and we also went sight-seeing on a double-decker bus around the whole of London. It was an enjoyable experience and the kids loved it.

From London, we travelled to Chicago where we visited my friend, Mrs. Dada. She took us and her kids to an amusement park and the kids absolutely loved it, they had lots of fun, candies, rides and really enjoyed themselves. We took pictures and they actually created a calendar with our pictures on it. We all rode the roller-coaster rides, except Oluwabusola because she was only two years old at the time. At that time, I was pregnant with the twins, but I did not realize I was pregnant until after we returned to Nigeria after the trip. We went round Chicago; their shopping malls to do some shopping, and the tourist attractions. They have quite a lot of high-rise buildings there, and my friend and her husband lived in the suburbs. It was a fantastic vacation.

On our way back from the United States of America, we had a stopover in New York, and we missed our connecting flight to Lagos, because there was a massive storm. We were supposed to take a flight from New York to London, but our flight was delayed due to the storm, so we arrived in London late. By the time we got to London, the British Airways flight we were supposed to board to Nigeria had left. So, we were stranded in London, and British Airways lodged us in a hotel at the airport for the night and booked us on the next flight to Lagos the following day. All in all, we had a nice time, and the children really enjoyed themselves.

I have never really travelled for a vacation by myself. I always travel with either my husband, my kids, or my friends. Hawaii is my dream vacation spot, I have never been there, and I would like to travel there. I have heard a lot about the place, that it is a warm place and very beautiful so I really would like to visit Hawaii.

EIGHT

Friendship & Love

My best friend is Jumoke Fabode (nee Ogunmilade). We met when we were in Form 1 in Secondary/High School back in 1964, and we have been friends ever since. When she got married, I was her maid-of-honor. My other close friends are Bola Animashaun (who I met at the University of Lagos), Kemi Beckley (nee Adejumo), and Linda Eribo (nee Osayi), who were my school mates at Fiwasaiye Girls Grammar School.

I have been in love twice in my life. The first time was with my ex-boyfriend, Segun, and the second time was with my husband, Adekunle. Before we got married, Adekunle and I were just good friends. We spent most of our courtship period apart; he was in the United States, and I was in Nigeria, and at that time, there were no cellphones. He only came home twice during the whole courtship period. I just saw in him the kind of person I could relate with, and I would want to live with because he seemed sincere, nice, and kind and plus I loved the way he relates with people and talks about people. I just saw that this man is a good man, and somebody that one can trust. I guess he fell in love with me during his last trip to Nigeria (during our courtship). Both our families knew each other before then and were supportive of the union.

It was after we got married, and came to the United States, and started living together that I actually fell in love with him. One of the things I observed about him was that despite the fact that some of his friends were doing some bad things, he did not join them. He is a disciplined person, he has his own principles, and he is someone one can trust. He is also a very kind person. Those are the attributes I saw in him that made me fall in love with him. It is not as if he has been a saint for the forty-four years that we have been married, he has his own flaws just like I have mine, but his good qualities far outweigh his weaknesses. Though one person I have been too forgiving with is my husband. I realize I have to forgive him when he offends me, because if you harbor any grudges against your life partner, you would not be happy, so the best thing is to forgive and move on so that your mind will be light.

Friendship rules

➢ Never put your whole trust in any man, but on God.
➢ Do not share your intimate secrets or issues (between you and your partner/spouse) with any friend, no matter how close you may be.
➢ Do not betray your friend's confidence; do not divulge their secrets to another person.
➢ Based on my life's experience, I would like to share some tips for getting through some tough situations in life:

Pray, put everything in God's hands.

Put all your problems in prayer and God will find a way out for you.

When you are having an argument with your spouse, it is better to keep quiet when tempers are still flying, so you do not say something you will regret which could escalate the situation. Try to be your normal self, until tempers have cooled down, and your partner has also calmed down.

Then pray about the situation, ask God for help and wisdom to handle the situation, and search your heart if you can find a cool way to express yourself, then you can discuss your concerns or the issues with your partner. But if you are still angry and you cannot find a civil way to communicate your concerns, give it time say a day or two and wait till you are calm and ready before discussing with your partner. If you are dealing with a Godfearing person, it makes things a lot easier.

When two people are quarreling or have a misunderstanding, and they call on you to mediate, you must pray, carefully hear both sides of the story before you say anything. There is no clear-cut way to resolve any issue. Try not to be biased or take sides, you must be impartial, and advise them to put everything in the hands of God.

NINE

The Inner Me

My favorite color is cream or light brown. I wear these colors but not so often, I wear them occasionally. I am pretty good at giving praise and compliments, but I do not flatter. I care a bit about what other people think of me, but I do not let it bother me much. The thing I do not like is when people get a wrong impression of me, but I guess in life, sometimes you cannot help that. I want people to take me for who I am, I guess that may not possible sometimes, particularly when people do not really know you that well. Generally, one should not let negative comments weigh you down. If you know you are guilty, try and improve yourself. And if you are not, continue believing in yourself.

I occasionally volunteer in church as a coordinator for the vacation bible school which usually holds annually in June/July during the summer vacation. I donate to charitable organizations like food banks, St. Jude Children's Hospital, and political parties. In church, myself and my husband donate non-perishable food items to the less privileged. We take them to church periodically, and from church, they are bagged and delivered to some shelters and homes.

My next-door neighbor to my left side is a ninety-six-year-old man who was widowed about five years back, and he has been living here alone ever since. His name is Kenneth, and he is a nice man. We attend the same church. To my right side, lives Mike and Jennifer, and there is a lady who lives opposite my house, her name is Peggy and she moved in about two years ago. She is very friendly, and she has a puppy. We are all cordial.

A good neighbor is someone you can call on if you need help, somebody who will take care of your things if he sees that something bad is going to happen to it. For instance, anytime we take out the trash and the refuse truck comes to empty the trash bins in our absence, Kenneth, my next-door neighbor will go out (after putting back his own) and put all our trash cans (including the other neighbors') back to where we usually place them behind the house. He does not have to do it, but he still does it anyway, which is very kind of him. He is a kind and friendly man.

The factors that have basically shaped my core values and affected the way I think, act, or understand the world are my religious upbringing and my mother. I was brought up to believe in God, be prayerful and read the bible always. My religious upbringing formed the basis for how I have lived my life. Also, my mother was my role-model because I watched the way she interacted with women from all spheres of life and background; both poor, rich, or working class. She also interacted with people warmly and was active in evangelism. I also observed the way my mum helped her relatives including the extended ones financially, even though she was not making much money. In fact, some of them lived with us at some point in time. All those things I learnt from them, and I took that into my marriage. It helped me accommodate my husband's relatives and my own relatives who came to live with us at some point in my marriage.

By nature, I am more of an introvert than an extrovert. I do not like making too many friends. I live a very private life. This is not to say I do not have friends, I have few close friends, but my children and my husband are my closest friends. The best day of my life so far was my sixtieth birthday party. I was just so happy that day. My children threw a surprise birthday party for me, and I was just so happy. Probably, my happiest day in my life is still yet to come. If I had no personal ties or obligation, I would choose to live in Nigeria, or where my children are.

The best job I have ever had was being a teacher, because I enjoy imparting knowledge into the upcoming future generation. The first school I worked at as a teacher was Victory College, Ikeja, Lagos, Nigeria. I also worked at Maryland Comprehensive Secondary School for so many years, before I got seconded to Ministry of Establishment, Alausa, Ikeja, Lagos. That was where I worked until I resigned from Government work and started my own business. All in all, I taught for eight years and I worked in the Ministry for about two years. I enjoy teaching very much because I love it when I teach my students and they do well in their exams. The success of my students brings me so much joy and motivates me to put in more effort into teaching and look for ways to make the students understand better what they are being taught.

Currently, most of the time, I am a stay-at-home wife, but I still do some administrative work at my husband's pharmacy from time to time. (few hours a week). The pharmacy is located at Baltimore, Maryland, United States of America. What I like about the job is meeting people and it keeps me busy and mentally alert.

I have quit a job before. I quit my job at Lagos State Ministry of Establishment back in Nigeria because I was made to work unnecessary long hours, without being compensated for it, even while I was nursing babies. It got to a stage when I just had my twins, and I was still in the hospital, that they brought some files to me at the hospital for me to work on. I then decided to venture into my own business. My husband and I decided that I should leave and start my own business.

Few lessons I learnt in my work life are as follows:

➢ Always be consistent in whatever you are doing.
➢ Ensure you do whatever you find yourself doing very well, try to be focused and not to make mistakes. Whenever you make mistakes, do not be too hard on yourself, but try to learn from your mistakes.
➢ Be friendly with everyone you are working with, so you can work along with them in a friendly atmosphere.

TEN

More on Marriage & Raising Kids

I have been married for about forty-five years now, and to be honest, it has been a journey. Staying married for this long is firstly by the grace of God, and by having a lot of patience, bearing in mind the lessons I learnt from my parents; how my mum was very persevering and patient with my Dad. I also lean on what the bible says about 'being submissive to your husband'.

One needs to put God first in everything, be tolerant, humble (with your husband and when dealing with your in-laws) and one must be tactful. Have the fear of God. Let God always be your guide and rule your heart always. 'The Lord is my Shepherd' Psalm 23verse 1 (KJV) has always been my personal mantra since I got married. Also, you need to be tactful in your interactions with your in-laws and in your marriage; knowing what to say and do at the right time.

You will also need to be very forgiving, able to let things go and let God have his way in your home if you want to preserve your marriage and home. When you make a life-long commitment before God, you should try to keep it, especially when there is no domestic violence involved. As time goes by, your spouse will gradually become like your sibling, since you live together and practically do everything together. As much as possible, also try to stay in the marriage because of your children (if you have any).

In most cases, when a marriage falls apart, the children suffer the most, they suffer both emotionally and psychologically. One would be giving them a wrong attitude or impression about marriage. So, we should endeavor be good examples to them, and to the others coming after us.

I would like to share a few tips on maintaining a healthy marriage by virtue of my own experience:

Try to take life easy, be forgiving, do not keep grudges and be open as much as possible with each other.

Whenever you and your husband are discussing an issue, which leads to an argument, once you notice that his tone has changed, the best thing to do is for you to stop talking. In some cases, he would ask you why you are not talking, but remain quiet. If, however he continues talking, let him talk. He may even say things that may annoy or provoke you but try your very best not to utter a word at that time. Eventually he would stop talking.

From my experience, I learnt that when that happens, silence is golden. Keeping silent for some time will give the both of you time to have a rethink and if he has said something to annoy you or more than he should say, he will eventually realize it and find a way to make up with you. And the same thing applies to you, the woman too.

For some couples, the man would either walk out or take his key and drive off (leaving the scene). I do not really subscribe to that because driving in anger could lead to an accident. But he can walk away from the scene to a different room or outside the house to cool-off. That is still okay.

Avoid repeating your husband's faults, particularly after he has apologized for it.

If your husband offends you, try your best to forget it and move on. If you feel the need to discuss it with your husband to get it off your chest, by all means do so, if it will clear things up. There is no man that is a perfect saint, well except for my father whom I can say 100% never had an extra-marital affair. As far as I know, men generally tend to be promiscuous.

If you discover any sign of extra-marital affair in your marriage, the best thing to do is to confront it and ask him whether it is true. He will most likely deny it. Explain point blank to him how you found out, and if he still denies it, remind him of your marriage vows (in church or court as the case may be) which you made to each other, and remind him of your love for him. This discussion may touch his heart and it may not. In some cases, it may touch his heart, and he will discontinue the affair, once he finds out that you know about it, except he is an unrepentant philanderer.

When you are close to God, these things will always be revealed to you one way or the other. It could be very painful, particularly when you are a chaste person, who never witnessed anything like that in your family growing up.

But what you need to do is to make up your mind to make your marriage work. Pray that God should take it off your mind, to be frank, it may not go totally from your mind, but pray so that it does not bother you so much.

Being a married woman does not mean you would not have men who will admire you and try to befriend you or lure you into a relationship, but you must try your possible best to always resist. When such thing occurs, do not make the mistake of telling your husband because men can be very jealous. They just cannot comprehend the idea of their wife having a manfriend or someone other than them in her life. If you tell your husband, he will be furious and even when you tell them that you did not encourage it, and you have been trying to avoid the person, they still will not believe you, and they will become suspicious. So, it is better not to tell your husband particularly if it is your husband's friend or someone he knows.

There was this guy – my husband's friend who toasted (made advances at me) me and I told him that it was not possible. He started off with compliments like 'You look beautiful'…'You look gorgeous', and then he came out straight and said, 'I would like us to be seeing each other'. This man is married with kids, and I told him point blank that it is not possible, and that I cannot be a dishonest and unfaithful wife, if he can do it, I cannot and I will not. He still tried his very best to pursue me further, and promised me heaven and earth, but I bluntly refused. I did not tell my husband until we relocated to the United States. There were also others who made such advances at me, but I never mentioned it to my husband.

When I eventually told my husband about the guy (his friend I mentioned earlier), my husband flared up and demanded to know the name of the person. I initially did not reveal it, but later after he kept insisting to know, I eventually told him the person's name, while explaining to him that the most important thing is that I did not accept his proposal, and I did not have anything to do with him, and that my dignity is still intact. Sometime after that, we met with the man and his wife, and my husband completely ignored him, it strained the relationship between them.

Reasons why you should not tell your husband are that it may strain the relationship between your husband and the other party, especially since you know they are friends, and your husband may start having doubts about you, which may in turn cause a strain in the relationship between you and your husband.

It is true that men think they have the liberty to flirt around, even after marriage, but it is not right. Men must caution themselves and maintain their fidelity and integrity with their wives.

Finally, when you are married, try not to deny your husband sex, anytime he asks because it is a sure way to drive your husband out. Unless you have a strong genuine reason such as severe sickness, or during menstruation.

The key word to balancing my personal and family life with my work life is simply 'Planning'. It requires a lot of Planning, Organization and Time Management. Organization is very key in your personal and professional life. The thing is if you are an organized person, it will reflect in your professional life too. While I was working at the Ministry, I was also doing my business on the side and managing my home at the same time. A woman should endeavor to be able to marry both her home and her career' that is the true definition of 'success'. One must not supersede the other. If you let one supersede the other, the marriage would either crack or it would not be a happy union.

Here are a few tips to juggling work with marriage and raising kids:

➤ As always, you need to put God first, pray for God to teach you how to go about the whole thing.

- You need to be able to manage and divide your time wisely; you have a home now so you must ensure you always have food at home. Prior to having children, you much ensure there is always enough food at home for your husband and housekeeper or help (if you have any).

- You also need to be very organized. Try to do your shopping (foodstuffs, groceries, toiletries, everything you know you will need for the month) either over the weekend or on your free day, so that you would not need to be shopping in bits or during your busy workweek.

- Over the weekend (for 9am-5pm workers) or on your off-days, ensure you cook different meals/stew/soups that you would need for the week, and then during the week, you can prepare anything you want to eat with the stew/soup such as rice, yam, eba (cassava flakes), fufu, etc. It will make things a lot easier for you.

- Along the way, children will come along so apart from work, cleaning and looking after your husband and the house, you would need to look after/take care of your children too. Normally, your husband should be able to assist you one way or the other, but in Africa, mostly the men do not. You just need to do it by yourself, meaning that:

- You may need to wake up earlier than your usual time in the morning, to bathe and clean the baby/children and get them ready for school, feed them breakfast, and prepare food for your husband and yourself before leaving for work. It requires a lot of planning and organization.

- There is the tendency for a woman to be very sensitive and edgy because of all these things such as having to wake up really early to look after your children and self, prepare food for everyone, and get ready for work. But you need to be patient with your husband and kids and learn how to manage stress in a healthy way.

- At times, you can ask your husband in a nice way, to assist you if you are feeling overwhelmed. Some husbands actually do assist.

> ➤ When you return from work, check the clothes that are dirty, and put them in the laundry basket, wash your hands, and then ensure you prepare dinner for everyone.
>
> ➤ Then try to take a nap or at least relax even if you do not sleep – just lie down and relax. You may take the nap before preparing dinner for everyone. If you return home before your husband, it is even easier to do this.

Before you know it, days will run into weeks, weeks will run into months, and then months will run into years. Before you know it, you will see that your children are all grown-up and your marriage has gone far, and everything is going well. Though there will be some hiccups along the way, but make sure you and your husband settle it amicably, without involving third parties if possible.

Raising my five kids has been a wonderful and rewarding experience for me. A few tips which helped me shape their values, morals and character are:

> ➤ They learn majorly by watching me all the time, since I am their first role-model. So, I ensure that I lay good example for them. Once they follow my example, they cannot go wrong, especially my girls. Once I tell them something is not right, and they follow my advice and example, they will not go wrong.
>
> ➤ When they misbehave or do anything that is not right, I correct them immediately.
>
> ➤ I do not allow them to mingle with bad friends. I try to know most, if not all their friends, and once I observe that they have friends that may lead them astray, I would advise them not to get involved with such person.

It all boils down to typically being a good role model, leading by example. It is what your children observe from you, that they would emulate. They watch your every move, your lifestyle, interactions with people, your morals, values, and they follow accordingly. It then shapes their own values, morals, character, and their lives as a whole.

ELEVEN

The Relocation

During the 1985 Import License Era in Nigeria, West Africa, when it was easy to import things from abroad to Nigeria, my husband and I were lucky to get an Import License. Getting an Import License is a legitimate way of bringing in finished pharmaceutical products from countries like Europe, India, China, Germany to Nigeria to sell. At that time, there were no manufacturing pharmaceutical companies in Nigeria, only packaging companies which only package finished goods imported from abroad. With the License, we were able to import goods directly from abroad to Nigeria, to sell at our pharmacy in Nigeria. I was also doing my own business on the side, so things were very buoyant for us. I had a plastic manufacturing company, where containers of pharmaceutical products were produced, to complement my husband's business. I bought my machines from Taiwan and rented a warehouse. From the time we wanted to install the machines, one of them fell, and so the machine gave us lots of problems until we eventually folded up the company. The government also imposed lots of taxes which did not make the business profitable. We put in a lot of manpower, money, and energy, but unfortunately, it did not yield much profit. Many factors contributed to our having to shut down the factory. The factory was run for about three years before we had to close it down.

A few years later, things became even more difficult because import licenses were not issued appropriately, and they were not issued to the right people. One had to go through a third or fourth party to get an import license. It is a license which had to be renewed annually. After some time, the government scrapped the issue of import licenses and encouraged indigenous companies to be manufacturing pharmaceutical products in Nigeria, which was not easy. Though we eventually diverted to manufacturing pharmaceutical products, but our income flow reduced drastically, and we still had a lot of responsibilities. Since then, things pretty much went downhill, I was still trying to make ends meet with my own business. I set up a travel agency, which I ran until I left Nigeria. Even when Adekunle's business was not going well, he diverted into getting diesel and supplying companies that needed it. But things were still going downhill for us financially, we still had children – the twins who were still yet to go to college.

Meanwhile, my elder brother, Adegboyega who lives in the United States with his family, used to visit us whenever he travelled to Nigeria. Being aware that Adekunle is a pharmacist, there was a time he came to the house, and observed that things were not really going well, no matter how we tried to make it seem like everything was okay. After he returned to the United States, he enquired from a pharmacist friend of his in the United States whether a person who studied in the United States and wants to come back to the United States, had a chance of finding a job easily. His friend the pharmacist confirmed that it would be very possible because pharmacists are presently in high demand in the United States particularly those who studied in the United States. Adegboyega then called me to inform me of his findings and encouraged Adekunle to travel to the United States to see the possibilities himself and make up his mind whether he would be willing to relocate.

Initially, Adekunle was reluctant to relocate, probably because his mother was still alive, and was very old. He was her only son, and they were very close. I then encouraged him to relocate and promised him that myself and his sister will take care of his mum. I kept my promise to him. There was no way we could all relocate at the same time, since our last born – the twins, were still in high school at the time. He eventually agreed to relocate with the agreement that he would first go, and then when the twins complete their high school education and WAEC exams two years later, they would also relocate to join him, and then I would be the last to go. Meanwhile, if we are able to raise the money, I would be visiting during the period of transition, before my final relocation, that was how the transition took place.

While my husband was away in the United States, it was not easy for me, I missed him, but I tried to keep myself busy with my business (the travel agency) and taking care of the twins. My first and second born, Olufemi and Olaide had relocated to the United Kingdom at the time, and my third born, Oluwabusola was studying at the Ogun State University in Ogun State, Nigeria at the time. Though she later joined us in the United States after she graduated, to do her Master's Program at Towson University. In July 2006, I relocated to the United States to join Adekunle, my husband.

When Adekunle arrived in the United States, it was not easy for him to get a job. He had to take some qualifying pharmacy exams; Naplex and English exams, even though he studied in the United States. He still had to pass those exams before he could be employed by anyone in the United States. It took him some time to pass those exams, though he was doing some part-time job on the side. His friend and a relative of his helped him to settle down.

By the time I joined him in 2006, he was already working in a pharmaceutical store. He started working as a full-fledged pharmacist, and from then on, we were able to rent a two-bedroom apartment in Vargis Circle, Windsor Mill, Baltimore where we all lived. From that apartment, we saved up and eventually bought a house in Parkville, Maryland. Meanwhile, while Adekunle was working, I was also working remotely as a sub-travel agent at a Travel Agency selling tickets.

TWELVE

Acquisitions and Prized Possessions

I buy things only as I need to. I am not an impulsive buyer; I do not shop on impulse, but very few times, I buy on impulse if I really like the item. For groceries, I must make lists before I go out to shop because I can be quite forgetful. It probably comes with age. My list ensures that I buy everything I need, without forgetting anything. I browse online both for inspiration and for pleasure. Sometimes, without having anything particular in mind, I browse and window-shop just for the fun of it. Most of the time, I shop only for necessities or because I know I might need the things soon.

There was a time I went out to shop at Macys and I saw this Calvin Klein blouse that I was not really planning to buy, but when I saw the blouse, I liked the style and I liked how it was cut. I looked at the price, it was quite high because it was not on sale, because I always get good bargain when I buy items on sale. Initially, I was a bit reluctant because of the price, but later, I said to myself 'I like this blouse and I am going to buy it because the blouse is really nice'. There are times when you see things like that, which catches your attention and you would not let it go, you just must buy it, except you cannot afford it. If it is not within my budget, I would not buy it. I try as much as possible not to buy things I cannot afford.

Five things I would save in a burning house are:

- ➢ My Bible
- ➢ My certificates
- ➢ My Gold Jewelry
- ➢ My Passport
- ➢ My other documents such as Credit/Debit cards, Social Security Number, etc.

Few lessons I learnt about the value of money from my family are:

- ➢ Do not let money rule you, you must always be in control of money. If you are earning $5,000 monthly, then your monthly budget should not be more than $5,000. Cut your coat according to your size always.
- ➢ When you start working or start running a business, let your spending budget always be within what you are earning from the salary or getting from the business as the case may be.
- ➢ Always save some money for contingencies or emergencies which may arise within the month.
- ➢ Ensure you also save a percentage or portion of your monthly earnings for the future, retirement or for any personal projects you have in mind.

These have shaped my values on money matters, and that is why I am contented with what I have. I do not compare myself with others, and I do not feel envious of anyone because I have learnt from my youth to be content with what I have. This is a great lesson, once you are content with what you have, you will never look at either a friend or someone else who is richer than you and be sad. You will always lead your own life and be happy.

I pay my bills on time, actually my husband, Adekunle and I receive joint bills and pay our bills together. You need to pay your bills because you have utilized the services.

If I had a million extra dollars, I would spend it on the following:

➢ I would donate majority of it to Charity, to help the less privileged.
➢ I would assist my children in any form, should they need the assistance.
➢ I would also assist my relatives and my husband's relatives financially.
➢ I would spend a small part of it to buy one or two things for myself such as:
    ➢ A vacation to Hawaii
    ➢ Some Gold Jewelry

THIRTEEN

Beauty Tips and Relaxation

I have been able to maintain my looks (looking younger than my age) only by God's grace. I use Aveeno or Jergens (Shea butter) body cream. I normally use Dial bathing soap or Dial anti-bacterial soap to bathe. I do not use bleaching or skin whitening cream because it damages the skin and causes more harm than good in the long run. Besides, I love my skin the way it is, and I am comfortable with my skin. I try to look good always, because I remember my mother always looked good, and I try to emulate her. I use very light make-up because I love the natural look and I always make my hair neat. I use straighteners to straighten it out or put it in rollers and set it. Sometimes, I plait it with extensions.

Six places I would like to visit in my lifetime are: Jerusalem, Hawaii, Disneyland, South Africa, Paris, and Italy. When I was younger, I loved travelling to different places. I still love travelling, but I do not do it as often as I used to when I was younger. I enjoy watching movies and reading fiction novels by John Grisham, Jeffrey Archer, Danielle Steel, Sidney Sheldon, Agatha Christie, and just funny books which one would read and laugh. I also like romantic books.

While living in Nigeria, I joined some associations such as Elites Ladies Club, which is a club that constitutes the wives of the Ago-Iwoye Elites Club (my husband's club in their hometown, Ijebu in Ogun State, Western Nigeria), Inner Wheel Club, which is also a women's club. The word 'wheel' in the name of the club represents the women's side of the Rotary Club. It is an all-women's club aimed at doing charity work, helping the less privileged. We used to visit and donate to the challenged children's home, seniors' homes, motherless babies' homes, hospitals, and schools. We once solicited for help in procuring four Dialysis machines from a Canadian Hospital, that is linked with another club. We made the request in order to donate the machines to a hospital in Nigeria that need them urgently. They agreed to donate the machines at no cost, but we had to pay the freight. So, we paid for the freight, and the machines were shipped to Nigeria, and we donated them to the Gbagada General Hospital in Lagos, Nigeria.

We try as much as possible to make life easier for the less privileged. During festive periods like Christmas, New Year or Easter, we donate foods, clothing and other items to orphanages, challenged-people's homes, seniors' homes so that they feel the impact of the season. Apart from giving them things, we used to cook food, snacks and eat with them, so that they will feel a sense of belonging, and feel the joy and merriment of the season.

I also love cooking. I like experimenting new recipes, I get that from my mother, because my mother taught me how to cook and bake. We used to bake our own bread, different kinds of cakes; cupcakes, birthday cakes, meat-pie, sausage rolls, and desserts such as cream caramel and so many other things.

FOURTEEN

A Retrospective

I am currently sixty-seven years old. The best year of my life was the year that I graduated from University – 1979, and the same year I had my first daughter, Olaide. I was heavily pregnant, still wrote my exams and passed excellently even though I was pregnant. Later that year, I had a beautiful baby girl. I had a lot to thank God for that year.

Getting older is good, but my prayer is that I grow older in good health. I do not want to get older and be sick. If getting older would be painful, I am not sure I would like that, but if it is going to be pain free, then I look forward to it. Though, I sometimes have some body pains which came with age. If one is in good health, growing older will not be scary. When I was younger, I could drive very long distance but now I cannot. I can still drive but my concentration has reduced, so it is safer for me not to drive long distance. I could dance very much for a long time when I was younger, but now I can only dance for a short time.

I am looking forward to seeing all my children established in their different fields, and my grandchildren growing up and visiting me from time to time. I want them all to grow up in the fear of the Lord.

Five things I would like to see, do, or accomplish before I die are:

- ➢ I want to remain close to God. I cannot compromise that for anything in the world.
- ➢ I want to see all my children married, settled and happy.
- ➢ I want to make a mark in the lives of some people.
- ➢ I want all my children to be close to God, though some of them already are.
- ➢ I pray and hope to have good health to enjoy the rest of my life.

FIFTEEN

Life Lessons for Young Women

Young ladies out there and reading this book, I would like you to know that you are beautiful. Do not let anyone ever tell you any different. Regardless of what you have been through, where you have been or what you are going through, you are Beautiful. Always remember that.

I would like to share some life lessons with you by virtue of my own experience:

> ➤ Regardless of your religious beliefs (Christian, Muslim, etc.), be close to God, and let God control your lives.
> ➤ When it is time to choose a life-partner, do not concentrate on his looks, whether he is handsome or good-looking, or what he has in his pocket, whether or not he is rich or poor.
> ➤ Look out more for the man's character and search your mind if you will be able to live with this man for the rest of your life. Will you be able to tolerate his behavior? Will his personality match yours or be compatible with yours?
> ➤ Study the character of the person you are considering marrying.

- Once you get married, you have to be fully committed. Never let yourself go, keep yourself attractive, possibly as you were before you got married.

- Humble yourself before your husband as the bible makes it clear that 'the husband is the head of the wife' Ephesians 5verse 23 (KJV) and wives must be submissive to their husbands as unto the Lord.

- Misunderstandings will come, but you must endeavor to submit to your husbands regardless, even when you know you are right. At that moment when the tension is high, just submit. Then later, when everything has calmed down, then you can explain yourself or the situation to your husband. It does not have to happen that same day.

- Marriage is a life-long commitment so you must be ready to bear everything that comes along with it except of course domestic violence (as it could be harmful to your life)

- As a woman, even if you earn more than your husband, do not ever let it get into your head, you should still be submissive to your husband. Respect is very important to a man. Besides, you never know what your husband can become tomorrow.

- Keep your marital vows, be faithful and satisfied with what you have. Even if your husband does not have much, 'cut your coat according to your size', and teach your children to be content with what they have too. They should not compare themselves with others.

- Finally, and most importantly, you must always put God in the center of your marriage and bring up your children in the way of God.

THE END

ABOUT THE AUTHOR

Boye Onalaja is a successful educationist, business woman, wife, mother and grandmother who has been able to successfully juggle work, business, marriage and raising kids together, without anyone of them suffering. In her interesting memoir, she shares her experiences and how she has been able to achieve this by the Grace of God, and also shares some valuable life lessons to the upcoming female generation.

Printed in the United States
by Baker & Taylor Publisher Services